New York City 1/17/11

flowing stone

For Diane,
as you read this verse
may the words fixed
upon the page as
firmly as stone begin
to flow with the
fluent music of
melodious poetry.

Other books by Garrett Buhl Robinson

<u>Poetry</u>

Martha (a poem)
Möbius Sphere

<u>Novels</u>

Zoë
Nunatak

www.garrettrobinson.us

flowing stone

poems

garrett buhl robinson

"A Sonnet for the Sonnet" first published in
Nomad's Choir Poetry Journal

"This is Grand Central, Mr. Robinson." is a quote from
"Aspects of Robinson" from *Poems 1947-1954,*
Weldon Kees

Table of Contents

One

Two

Three

Four

Five

I Sing

— Walt Whitman

.

One

Whispering Emily

I have been damaged
for this I blame no one
I blame my enemy
oblivious ignorance
that senseless
part of all of us
awaiting the numberless
ways of awakening

Yes, I am damaged
but I am not destroyed
outgrowing my thick skin
there is no end to my opening
spanning the cleaved severities
arching between ripe seasons
knowing if nothing more
life is what I live for

Sylvia

I offered the abundance
of my fruit's sweet nourishment
that our mutual needs may
grow appeased with dispersed seeds
but you stripped me of my leaves,
lopped off my limbs, ripped up my roots
and abandoned me because I no longer produce
yet I still do.

None Other

One has no tribe. One is with everyone
        and one is alone.
One takes nothing except the dendritic
        path one makes oneself.
One ascends but not upon a charnel heap
        of others' defeat,
one climbs not upward, but outward beyond
        the lines of limits,
the frays that converge in oblivion
        at one's unseen reach
where one gains one's grasp with one's release
        vastly broadening
one's open composure, a gathering
        in being gathered.

August 7, 1974
— For Philippe Petite

Unburdened as the sky it treads within
the foot of the hind step lifts. On the tip
of an arc drawn by the sweep of his leg
hinged from the hip of him fixed in suspense,
a dimple on the cheek of the breathless,
framing the void he traverses and seals,
his pinioned toes outstretch in deft balance.

The sole of his foot floats attentively
listening with a taut tuning of nerves
inlaid and refined an entire life time.
Above the din of the world, he only hears,
with his whole body and being, the plum
equilibrium within his ear.
He accepts this fine and delicate note
as the gift of his existence, knowing
this solitary and continuous
line can take him anywhere he desires.
His world is the wire, all else is distraction
offering broad palms of treacherous taunts
to beguile his life distilled into one
step, the only step from the beginning till
the end — the step being made — the perfect
step on the perfect path.

                              Unfaltering,
the feather light step plumed with elegance
is rigidly quilled with sleepless practice
as in the night he tightwires through his dreams,
then awakens with the shift of his weight
into a new day, a new beginning,
a new note on his fretless instrument
deepening the past, ascending ahead,
playing the string that sings complete with his
dance warbling harmonic.
                              The bow pitches
slowly and bends to the quivering tips
in a compensating sway that pulsates
between the skitter of birds twitching tails,
swirling between perches, encircling and
broadening with helicopters above
an ocean of gaping, glistening eyes
transfixed, focused on him unwavering,
walking through stark naked space, his vision
concentrated on threading the high wire
between an equal sign of earth and sky
through a needle's eye to fulfill the day's
unsurpassable achievement – to be
the one who complements the monuments.

Lift and Turbulence

Over the frozen surface of a bone dry sea
my feet clamored on sliding steps plashing through the
sands as I ran, cresting a wave of the worried
dunes at Kitty Hawk. Here as a child I had spied
with my own eyes an event impressed indelibly
on my mind – from the curved surface of the
Earth, the shore of the sky where millions of dreams
were wrecked, this one had been gloriously received.
Waving my arms I ran to a man imploring —
"Did you see? Daedalus' myth has been achieved,
the task that stumped all the modern Archimedes,
the desire spanning the entire human history,
now just as the birds, just as the angels, we have wings.
The path of mankind has risen into the sky."
The man turned his head, spit, then said, "I don't believe it."

Corpus Delicti

My body is my work
that you may interpret.
Composed from exposure
livid experience
breathtaking altitudes
and fathomless depths
drawn from my head and breast,
I withhold nothing

with lavish abundance.
This is my gift, this me,
my open offering.

The one thing I conceal
is the tread of my feet
which I have made of thieves.

A Momentous Notice

I originated from an event
of unsurpassable magnificence
that does not have a single precedent
and is far beyond all comparison.
It is an event of significance
that is the essence of consequence
more complete than everything in each instance
in the seamless sequence of continuance,
the fathomless beginning without end,
the event with only one witness —
everything for all time and all existence.
This event is the universe's origin.
I am no different than anyone else.
We are all the same. We are all unique.

Two

In a Bridge

> — For Dennis Brown: teacher, mentor and friend.

I exist because I am, because I
span. I am always crossing this river.
I only cross this river for everyone.
I strut in humble function, riveted
with loaded and balanced beams sternly still,
providing and extending a smooth surface,
a silent yet lyrical transversal
plucked with the notes of each passing person
thrumming above the long song of water.

I stand firm in the current. Roads combine
and overlap upon me, then diverge
afterwards, dispersing at the other
side of where they arrive. All the time I
see each traveler in the same way — unique.
Together we make a straight path that turns
an obstacle into a scenic highway.

I watched as you approached. I will watch you
disappear. In this segment of your life,
now, as you pause to reflect on the river
you may feel how all the accomplishments
of the past and all the future's potential
converges within you. Only you can
know this for yourself. As for me, I know
I am and for the length I span, you may pass.

Orogeny

Our nipples are scars from our ancestors
huddled together in burrows beneath
the lizards' massive feet and ripping claws.
The scars are from the nuzzling young feeding
on the sleeping adults, hungrily nibbling
through the darkness at the soft undersides.
The long, surviving line of our mothers
were the only ones who would endure this,
the only ones who could not bear us to starve.
From their pain and their kindness, they made milk.

Musical Platitudes

This couldn't be about me, at the least,
not exclusively, but I often hear
that I have lost. I would agree except
this is impossible. After all what
have I ever gained? My complete release
is not only inevitable, it
is continual, if I ever gathered
anything together in the first place.

If I had any loss, it would not be
the loot of avaricious aggressors,
those figures making the snaggle-toothed maw
of a monstrous emptiness embodied
by a presumptuous non-existence.
My loss could only be everyone's gain.
We do not fall apart. We diffuse
our illusion of distinction.

Those portions of our existence which we
assimilate into our sense of self,
the body which facilitates being
just as being forms the bonds upon which
we swing, revolving in spontaneous
arrangements, while we elastically cling,
waltzing as we sing in pulsing bodies
leaping between pairings, assured by our

feelings found in the touch of another,
are always in unison, as ever
present, extending the infinite,
by contributing to the immediate.

Musing

An image of music while sitting in silence.
A room appears, opening with a soaring ceiling.
Raised drapes completely cover the windows and spill
lavishly over the smooth and polished parquet.
Standing atop a piano, a candelabra
raises numerous palms extending tiny
torches flickering as glistening beads of wax
that freeze like petrified weeping. Chopin sits brooding
over the keys, touching the notes and taut wires
quivering with nimble experiments fluttering,
naturally settling into melodies till
the petal releases the held tones, receding
into the source, building for another surge,
continuously within yet only heard
in alternates through which the inventions emerge
as the arrangement is sequenced to be released.

Divertimento

Two strangers approach on a busy street,
just a single step before their paths meet,
where they veer aside to pass, however
the choice each chooses matches the other
so that they shift from one foot to the next
then suddenly stop, standing breast to breast,
staring in astonishment face to face
so that they simultaneously say:

"Don't we complement one another's life,
so disinclined to pass each other by."

Needless to speak, needless to say: silence,
I stand by myself in consternation
when personal interaction becomes
a dismissive, digressive distraction.

Se Offendendo

Ophelia's lifeless flight, a clear image
beneath the slate surface of a still lake.

After the emotional uproar
of play upon intricate play parried
on an arranged stage of rapacious rage
where ghosts, greed, jealousy and other vacancies
bled a cast of costumed corpses who bowed out
and teetered and toppled the sprawling red curtain
as the prince, the relentless progeny,
the seeker of truth, torn and confused, plumbed
the retched depths of bitter life and death —
the stained sword clatters down the stone steps.

Ophelia's curtsied immersion,
the pallid shivers of a riffling brook.

Aubade that Made the Day

Poetry makes nothing happen.
— W. H. Auden

Touching the keys with her fingertips
she opens a space on a blank page
as if turning a corner
into an unexpected place
while her serif steps lead the way
through dimensions of invention
shining with the life of her mind,
increasing without consuming,
broadening without displacing

— pure creation.

Snow Shapes

I have heard it said,
or perhaps I have
read, that each one is
completely unique,
but I must confess
I have not as of
yet been able
to verify this.
Of course Mr. Hume,
we mustn't assume.

However I do
know that when they form
and take crystal shape
symmetrically
arranged, every limb
each one extends is
exactly the same.
It baffles me how
the unique is achieved
with such regularity.

Ascending the Ridge at the Horizon

It is no surprise that discouragements
are prolific from the lips of cowards.
Those who see little possibility
within the clutter crowding their chambers
have no space to spare, yet still they try dragging
others in. If they see no change within
their petrified lives, allow them to serve
as the foundation on which others rise.

So if they say, *Give it up*. You may say
Yes, as I climb. If they say, *You have gone
too far*. You may say, *Yes, to be enclosed
within your provincial conventions*.
If they say, *You're out!* You may say, *because
I am too big to fit in.* If they say,
You're dull and blank. Tell them to back away
to broaden their scope for the magnitude
of your features. If they say, *You're history*.
You may say, *Yes, because history is
made of people like me*. And if they say,
There isn't a chance. You may say, *What need
of chance when I have my will*. Best yet, speak
with the grandeur of your accomplishments.

Personal Piece

This may be the first work where I confess
the speaker to be me. I often hide
behind my prosaic prattle, disguised
in the multiple personalities
crowded within my mind. Don't be concerned
though, I don't consider this a mental
malady, rather it is a social
necessity, my multiple person-
alities keep me company. I have
often suspected the reason behind
the labor in my expressions' designs
revolve around the fact that I lack
the skills to perform in person, and then
I remain detached from the involvements
assembled in other people's awareness,
snipped by the limits of their perceptions.
From my diverse personal opinion
though, the misconceived personalities
that populate their sense of you and me
are by far the most dangerous delusions.

Primordial Courtship

Ever since we met, introduced in circumstance, we danced in circumspect.
Our demonstrations were offered admissions. Our evaluations were playful evasions.
When we walked, our favorite destinations were each other's surprise, one leading the other
along paths of discovery departing from all else into the secret of ourselves, finding our most
cherished place was anywhere together.
We carefully noted each time our directions diverged by the gentle tugging of our linked fingers
and each time we bumped into one another and tumbled in comfortable conversation.
Then in one unforgettable instance, beyond the assessments of our standings,
or the firmness of the seats from which we assert ourselves, or the prospects
with the completion of each loop of our separate involvements
and the yields with which we may return together,
we stop talking and close our eyes
from all we see and all we seek,
and lean toward one another
for the pure sense
of our tenderness
in the touch
of a kiss.

Made of Inspiration

I have slogged through the miasma of bogs,
twisted my body through gnarly forests,
rose upon the mountains as they amassed,
tumbled into and through confluent streams
and dipped myself in oceanic pools
as I found my life along diverse paths
but the most awesome feat I've ever seen
is that of an epiphytic orchid,
tenuous and tenacious on a bough,
glistening with dew and made out of thin air.

Qualifying Quantity

What can be counted
when there is only
one of everything?

Regarding a case
particularly
bewildering, if
there is such a thing
as identical twins,
why do we give
them different names?

Considering this
I happened to find
myself perplexed in
a number of ways.

Individual Incidents, Inseparable Ever Since

I.

Truman stands next to the crest
of the steps at Grand Central
Station astonished to see
a river running upstream.

II.

Susan bumps into some boys
smashing acorns to see what's
inside. Pausing in shock, she
points out the oak overhead.

Pastoral

Following the road twisting through the country,
whipping through the utility's cleave through the trees,
taking an arrow's flight over the ravines,
I pass a pen plotted along the roadside,
a narrow enclosure of hoof stamped stubble
lined with twisted barbs of wire strung along dead limbs
lifting them. A beautiful horse with a shiny coat stands,
his muscular body twitching with biting flies buzzing in clouds
stirred with the swishing swats of his tail. His head turns,
not following me behind the flashing glass or the liquid luster
of paint, but following the passage, a blaze between somber
    eyes.

Ditty Indeed

Consider that most of the time
people throwing dirt in your face
are simply digging their own graves
and although you may be so kind
to bear the brunt to change their mind
you have to let them have their way.

After reading some poems by Czeslaw Milosz

For what it is, it is worth.
As ever, I never intended doing damage
and didn't
but watching you walk away and seeing
the tenderness of your now delicate steps
I should not need to confess the obvious,
the best explanations are demonstrations,
but if it is not already known —
I am compelled to compose.
That time, where else was I to engrave my lines
but on the soles of your feet
while you tried to trample me?

Accomplishing the Ongoing

On seas of uncertainty,
propelled with inspiration,
extending in dimensions
with every encounter,
my craft, my vessel sails.

The tools are the materials.
The materials are the tools.
The product is the process,
the activity, the engagement.

Creation is the destination,
discovering the possibilities
arranged over horizons
on the crests of the tumultuous.
Success is continuance.

Inspired by Richard Sennett's *The Craftsman*.

Fulcrum

Between the indistinct lengths
of the blurred future
and the past thickening
in immobile stone I stand
in precisely the same place
where Archimedes said
he could move the world and he did.

There is no crossroad.
There is no graphed path.
Here is the moment,
the immediate,
and what is made of it.
Here I ascend the stairs of my study
as I rise in spires of my mind.

Consideration is Non-Dismissive

I have heard it said,
both through the guiding enlightenment of sage advice
and through the memorable lessons of personal experience:
treasure keeps company with difficulty.

Is the difficulty required of the value?
Or does the value appreciate through the difficulty?

Often the recognition is gained through others' attention
curiously crowding around the obvious where competition
ensues between collective agreement and individual obtainment.
Sometimes the recognition is through the individual's attention
discovering the luster beneath evasive obscurity.

All is worthy.
Merit is existence.
Value is affection.

Tiles of Text

This path is fabric,
a weft of a voice,
a narrative line
weaving between
the identities
the warp signifies.
Often, solitude
serves as the loom
from where the bolt rolls
undulating waves
stilled with your step
on a path composed
of being composed,
of being woven.

Three

The Stupid Truth

Throwing a tantrum
from a grocery cart
a child outlines
the mind's stemming
development before
realizing the world
existed before him
and only a mother
will trouble with his
spastic pouting —
"It's just the stupid
truth."
         I have never
once heard this before
but it astounds me
with sensibility.
The truth must be dumb,
as dumb as the moon,
as dumb as the sun.

Robin Hoodlum

Jesse James
thought he was clever
giggling, clutching
a bag of cash
in one hand
cocking a pistol
with the other
robbing a bank
robbing a family
robbing a wife
robbing children
robbing life
blank point
shot the clerk
in the face

Broken Stone

Reading an old book I could not help but think
how the inconceivably incongruent
consistently fits together and I considered
the impossibility of consciously accomplishing
this, and then I closed my eyes to see
a shattered ridge of rock cinched by the sky.

Walking through the woods I paused once
and unwittingly watched a dead trunk
left in the shade of the others' growth
slowly tilt and topple in its own time.
There was a dry cracking and a creaking moan
then a thud that rasped to a rest in dropped leaves.

I accept that I will never be like I was
before, so I have decided to be better.

Bridge

She feels to be
the tuning keys
at the fretted tip
of an instrument
where the strings
tautly extend
into a misty distance.
The plucking instance
of experience
along with the strumming
chords of arrangements
make the music
of harmonic
accompaniment.

Title

Beyond what is intended for the audience,
set on the verge of obscurity
pressed to the tip of a wing
clipping the view of most of the stage
yet offering a peak behind the scenes
between the side skirts fluttering
in anticipation and preparation –
the cheapest seats in the theater
afford the opportunity to witness
the deep breaths and the relaxed release,
then the transformation of the dancers
as they step onto the stage.

Starting from Scat

If you stop upon the start of my script
and see it trailing off in the distance,
know that it is a story without return.
The wide open may feel liberating,
but it is also empty. There are no
obstacles, but neither is there shelter
and in such a desolate place the only
path one may take is the path one creates.
I have grown accustomed to discomfort.
My companion is ever true solitude.
I accept that to arise in the new
I must plunge into the unknown.
The blazing, audacious leap for the stars
is a long, frigid embrace of the dark.

All in All

It is easy to think of myself as drowning,
immersed in the surfaceless expanse
of not water, but the enigmas of existence.
There is no foothold. There is nothing to grasp.
The world eludes me yet will not release me.

Then in my most inexplicable state I call
awareness, I call wakefulness, dismissed
from the oblivious conviction of slumberous
dreams, I consider how I make a cast
of myself with the most impeccable realism
each time I slide into a bath, or dive
inside a lake, or wade through the waves
while wondering what displacement I make
is worth noticing on the blue on blue horizon.

Another Lesson

I.

I am not sure if I am
chasing my demons
or if the demons
are chasing me
or if we are just
circling and screaming.

II.

Deciding to rid
myself of these shadows, I
plunged into the sun.

Manhattan

Off to my job I pause at Bryant Park
as a woodpecker skitters from tree to tree
then hammers for grub assiduously.
The traffic passes and the people crowd
and the bird pauses from chipping the bark
to wonder what all the hubbub's about.

En Pointe

On the pinioned steps of the firmament,
thundering with the rapture of gliding silence,
streaming over the stage of a dark lake
with the willowy waves of spectral grace,
the swans rise from the horizon of dawn.

Distance per Day

Through the sliding glass door
I see the deck's steps descend
into the garden.

The swaying fronds of ferns
and the broad palms of leaves
flow over the railing.

The outstretching trees balance
at the surface of the earth
and flat stones plop a path
that sinks into a living sea.

Catching myself leaning
into a long, dreamy lapse
I see how the tranquil day
takes place at the speed of light.

Page d'un Livre

Years ago, listening to a recording,
I learned the centuries old folk tale told
in Paris about "The Sunken Cathedral"
that rose from the Seine on unforeseen nights.
The trilling of the piano piece shaped
spires climbing from the sudden stillness of water,
floated ponderous stones and trickled notes
streaming down the sides of winged majesty
that glowed through the spectrum of windows.
I was seized with the ecstasy of understanding.
Now staring at a page's murky surface,
the fleck of letters, the stir of words, the drift
of phrases and the course of composure, I see
Claude Debussy touching the keys of poetry.

An Education

Poetry's a type of childhood
reminding me of the playful
day when I first saw a paper
airplane. Before, I had always
lived a rock drop existence,
the abrupt and inevitable falls
and how everything broke.
I would topple and toss over
the knowledge of loss.

Then, in the abounding space
of an auditorium, I watched
a classmate meticulously fold
a simple sheet of paper
and then reached up to set
it in the air where it floated
in flight and I followed
it with my eyes in delight
of lift and loft.

Rm. 506

In the sound of the lively city outside
those nights spent soaking in a bath come to mind
as suddenly as realizing the water has turned cold.

The surged gurgle of immersed movement
The tinny porcelain drip
The plunk of the plug being pulled
The lowering line of exposure
The startling sound of the drain's slurp

I follow each trickle with my fingertip
until I find the tub has turned bone dry.

About Books

Some may say their ordered ranks on the shelves
are columns supporting themselves, levels
arising through the structures of instruction.

Some may say their stylized covers
entice with entrancing offers
for the subscription of any attention.

Some may say the authors and the titles
command, impress and direct their respect
with the authority of their subjects.

Personally, the bindings, the pages,
the who and what are incidental to me.
Even the words seem slight and typified.
Rather, my interests are in the passages
that take me anywhere I can imagine.

JB

It has been said that nice guys finish last,
but such texts are taught in schools without class.
Lack of expenditure is its own limit
depleted with tepid diminishment
and what lacks more of its own than indifference?

Those who continue even when harassed,
those who find fulfillment beyond their caste,
those who endure after their hopes are dashed,
those who can sing even while being lashed,
those who see the use after being trashed,
those of beauty being bruised and bashed,
those taunted yet are not craven or crass
are most capable for the noble task.

The lesson's done, there's no question to ask,
The truth is that nice guys are built to last.

In Memory of Officer Peter Figoski, NYPD

At the bottom of a trough of a depressed day,
I read about police cars racing upstate
to pick up the daughters of an officer
who had been fatally shot while confronting
the truly disturbing from which any other
person would flee. An officer and a father
lost his life for doing an honorable job.

I felt like someone standing on a bridge
in the thick benefit of the social flow.
Then I heard a ruckus and peeking
over the railing, noticed transgressive groups
chipping away at one of the columns.
The whole structure shifted and groaned
while they maniacally laughed below.

After shuttering the store at the close of day,
I returned to the boxed room of my residence
where I carefully arrange my own interest
to patch together the interior of a home.
Sitting at my desk, I am impressed by
the imposing coldness of oblivion
and the relentless sense of the void.

I will never forget that this emptiness is
the overwhelming imperative to continue.

Autotelic

Dismembered from remembrance, I think I
am not where I would like to be, but I
know such places are mirages. I
know they exclusively reside in my
imagination and the only place I
can be found is designated as the
irreplaceable realm of myself. I
know, at least for me, there is nothing else. I
must be my own place of progress. I
am my only sustained development. I
acquire nothing but understanding. I
am engaged in my refinement where I
am realizing exactly what I
am so I may more fully offer what I
may become in all there is to be and
through this, give myself completely.

For a Lady

I could watch her enter a room for the rest of my life.
The air electrifies with her arrival, the suspense of her
feather steps hush any crowd until everyone
is set at ease as she graces a seat.

She privately repeats to me, "Ne comprenez-vous pas?"
inflecting the question in countless ways:
amused, pouty, urgent, incredulous,
teasing every angle to elicit a response.

I am not sure what I do in agreement.
Her soft fists playfully pounding my chest,
the movement of her lips, the brilliance in her eyes,
her surprise, her smile, the refreshment of her endless interests.

I may know little and less of how and what she says,
but what matters most is knowing why she speaks.

Holiday

She has outlived everyone.
All her family and friends stand
on tables in polished frames
where only her dreamy eyes
can coax them back to life.

The city is her last
companion often extending
from its insensitive mass
a compassionate hand to
lift her heaviest days.

The holidays are tough though,
with everyone sharing their
homes and phones with family,
drawing in their kith and kin,
those they hold most close.

Then, she is surprised to find
her favorite magazine has
arrived early, filled with poems
and perspectives in the wondrous
comfort of a familiar voice.

It is a dear friend returning
from worldly travels with whom
she is delighted to savor
every delicious detail
the entire, undisturbed day.

Intercourse and Offspring

The meadows are for lovers. Let them be.
They are delicate beauty. Let them roll
sumptuously in the sweet luxuries
of one another, meandering along
shores of glittery drifts and softest sway.
They are the luscious unfolding of flowers,
the buzz of mellifluous bees and ripe
fruit dripping from the limbs of trees. They are
exquisitely pleasing, the emblems
and reality of nature agreeing.

The arduous travails are for others,
for the resolute, intrepid and bold,
those in whom indomitable life grows
for the glory of honorable victories.
To lift laboriously from the sumps
of despondence, to struggle from within
the shadowy valleys and ripped ravines
deeply gurgling empty echoes
of the sifting wash drowning the topples
of pulverized defeats, to rise from these
debacles of icy agony,
to clamber over shattered boulders shaken
from the lost rocks of the granite fog,
treading the pathless slope against resistance,
guided by what is most difficult,
and burst through the obscure blindness
as dawn upon the mountains
and pour forth to fill the seas.

The Gift

He was given a boulder.
He was stuck to a stone.
He has rolled upon it
less often than the times
its crushing weight
has rolled over him.
But to leave it
and run with others
would be to abandon
what he is.

He has yelled at it.
He has beat his head against it.
Then through the years
by grinding and gnawing,
he learned to work it.
He must heave
to turn its dumb,
encumbering stubbornness
upon a balance
he has built.

Then, in a fixed spin,
it throws a teeny spark
he catches in his cupped hands
and tenderly kindles
the growing glow
that he lifts and scripts
in dancing flames
to emblaze the page.

Four

Ever Day
    — For Kenneth Koch

Before arriving in New York I wrote the lines,

>Truman stands next to the crest
>of the steps at Grand Central
>Station astonished to see
>a river running upstream.

The turn of events continued to amaze
as I found myself in Grand Central Station
selling electronic readers, not that literature
had become robotic, although there have
been countless campaigns to accomplish this
through history. Rather, we have simply
returned to tablets, with binary circuitry
for cuneiform on palimpsests of digital
memory randomly accessed by our interests
and providence along the lines arranged
in techno bios of consoles and manifolds
of our conglomerations together
in the adherence of custom and convenience.
I stood describing to a lady a book of my own,
suspending our engagement with a mixture
of my urgency and her patience
in the stream of transit passage
in an aorta of the city, explaining my reason
for naming the protagonist after Weldon Kees
and then quoting the lines in a tone
affecting incredulous sadness,
"This is Grand Central, Mr. Robinson"
and then expressing my astonishment
with the rosy cheeks of naivety
in an expletive attempt to angle agreement,

"Isn't that an uncanny coincidence?"
And she deliberated as immovably
beautiful as the Himalayas,
"What we think of as coincidence is just
evidence of our subjective perspective."
And I began gathering the pieces of my
shattered beliefs and reassembling
the instance with the sense of my new existence.

Transmission from Planet Platitude

We may measure life in length,
of transpiring time and survival
of our accomplishments' endurance
after compacting hands have crumbled.

We may measure in breadth
of our circumstance spanning
the circumference in which our
desiring eyes are satisfied.

We may measure in depth
from the pools of the present
cloud flung and sprung forth
in the tippling drift of the current.

However, being that life is organized
not as much from intention
and more from the unexpected
consider the measure of arrangement

not enclosed with obtainments
but encompassed with openness
realized in intricate correspondence
and sustained by continuous change.

Turns of Attention

As an alternate to Eliot's
imperious explanation of
the scholarly study required to excite
the aging imagination, I prefer
envisioning Yeats as he did it,
pacing the top of his tower unconcerned
with any time except eternity
while enrapt in overlapping interests
of intersecting fields extending in
dimensions more numerous than the infinite
as his life continues to rise
with the minds he inspires.

Cognition

The creative touch of conversation
is astonishingly common
yet the miracle can only be
diminished in inattention.

I am numbed with amazement as I listen
to others revolving through thoughts
in a constantly evolving environment,
surging through the sequence of the mind's
experience, building the momentum
to leap into the openness upon every arising
topic erupting from their enlivenment together
as they mesh their interests in engagements
that whirl with the wonders of involvement
through an endless discovery of one another.

Two Men

Many have spoken of Michelangelo standing
for weeks staring at a block of marble
where the potential of countless sculptures
moved with ease, yet, where only one David
stood and still stands, precocious and resolved,
full of song and indomitable life
and with little more than a strip of leather,
a stone and his God faced the raging giant
who cleaved his people from peace.

Rodin scooped globs of wet clay together
then carefully searched for an idea,
adding and subtracting in a balance
between a seat, a person and posture,
assembling a figure sitting on a stone
with a ponderous head propped on his elbow,
less individual, more involvement,
accumulating contemplation of
the past in the present from a smashed caste.

Forms

Vivid music distilled on the page,
figures of dancers upon the stage,
every letter a sculptured instant
that makes the expressive arrangement
along the measured steps of the lines
that spring to life in the reader's mind.

This Enchantment

After abandoning hope for response
I am fully committed to writing
whether without an audience or friend
or wandering through the wilderness again.
Only composition can compose me.
And if I am fixed to a deluded
distance and dispatched upon the attachment
of dreams, I accept this whole heartedly.
For are these dreams not drawn forth from the mind,
and from where else can our lives find meaning
but at the seat of our understanding?
Yet as I write and reach, checking my mail
feels like a blast of an icy draft,
a vacuum pushing in from oblivion.

Maieutic

Impulsively, from some innate inclination
for preservation - cohesion through repulsion,
he felt enflamed with hate for another.

Before stoking the raving flames,
before stepping into the furnace,
he paused to consider that if he hated
this person for what this person is,
he is hating a person for being a person,
and is he not a person too?
Then must he not hate himself?

So he thought, he must hate that person
for something that person has,
or for something that person lacks.

But considering this, he wondered what
that might be, and furthermore, why this
would elicit such a powerful sense of apprehension.
So he thought, what I must hate is what I do not
comprehend about this person, so with this, he asked
this person what this might be,
and they fell in love with understanding.

A Day's Accumulation

Gathering gravel through the dragging day
then plopping exhausted in the chair at home,
slowly, he begins picking off the rocks,
feeling the sharp pocks dented in his skin.
The first ones drop with a clatter, then thuds
deepen in the holding bowl, a tumbler
he turns while mulling through his thoughts,
churning in conversation with his wife
until she pulls them out one at a time,
river stones polished as smooth as her hands,
and sets them in a row to shore
the water that flows between them.

Facts and Figs

The mistake I made where we met
from different directions of the unexpected
is — I smothered the delight of surprise
by seeking something more distant than your eyes.

I was walking through a museum
eternally contemporary,
as every creative instance
is immediate attention,
but instead of my brushing features
teasing intricacies in elaborate interactions
I searched for a professor or doctor
to lecture me on my own biology.
Without a smile, I knew no gladness.
Without tears, I could not feel sadness.
I searched for figures and ignored the source,
groping for explanations while we held hands.
The mistake I made, was making a mistake.

Exam

Having spent days of weeks
and weeks of years
and years of his life
that to his astonishment
continue to multiply,
he only notices
the passage of time
in skipping increments
when he lifts his head
from studying the various
ways blots of ink
can be arranged on a page.

On occasional necessity
he journeys to the store
and along his jaunts
of wandering thought
he suddenly stops
at an arrangement
of rocks displayed
at a critical angle
in the corner of his eye.
With no intention
he discovers an arrangement
of infinite proportions
as he pauses in awe.

In this, what he sees
is that through all his
reading miles of lines
throughout his lifetime,
not the information,
but the intensity
of the engaged activity
has sharpened his attention
to discover the wonder
of the immensity
of possibilities
in any given instance.

NYC, Poetry and Prosperity for All

A mountain made by hand, spanning every
reach of humanity, where the greatest
accomplishment is not a physical
feature, even from the towering spires
that touch the stars in each uplifted eye,
but in the sustained activity
of boundless diversity engaged in
every means of human interaction
imaginable, all effort meshing,
not into a machine, but a living being,
an entity of restless unity.

The buildings stand in patient observation
with the twinkling lights of the life inside,
as endless passages of rivers flow
in which every particle is sentient,
consciously contributing to the current
while turning into the refreshment
of each gently creasing rivulet
splashing from the fountains of every interest
pouring from the accumulating sources
billowing into breathtaking heights that rise
in columns lifting the whole world wide.

They talk, often

Grocery lists, places and names
evoking renditions of each existence
they alternately trade as they communicate
in the ways they arrange their life together.

Often, their speech flows with casual ease,
murmurs and gestures of comforting pleasure,
or witty flips of fruit they pick from passing trees
to share with giggling nibbles until their lips sweetly
meet or stern statements of stone walled ways they intend
only for passing.

Often, the words have little more meaning
than the planks along the boardwalk
as they hold hands and stroll
into every day's sunset together.

> — Dedicated to the intended audience of Dylan Thomas'
> poetry.

While You Read

I am diligently devoted
to figuring out how to write
a poem that will reach up
from the page and place a bright
and perfectly ripened cherry
in your mouth just to see you smile.

I think I'm getting closer.

Mythic City

At a wall-less arch of a door-less gate
is an opening to a wondrous place
that welcomes each individual walk
and speaks as friends in every way we talk.
The inns offer sumptuous comforts for rest,
or if you wish, revelry for merriment.
The markets extend from every doorstep
where respectful desire is satisfied
with abundant buyers for everything
for in such abundance there is every need.
In the plaza's center a column stands
with inscriptions everyone understands
that uplift eyes with inspiring lines
of poetry spiraling into the sky.
And the bell towers musically chime
at every instant of the timeless time.
And every song has a rapt audience
and there is always a performance
for the whole place is a theater's stage
where all are encouraged to play
and everyone has a special part
in the role of being just who they are.
And the sleepless city is always rising
as the buildings being built are climbing,
arranging with every way we interact
in the patterns through which we gather.

Apartment

The mist quickly thickens in the distance.
I cannot make out the building next door.
Unsticking the window, I lift the pane
        and the fog pours into the room,
spills over my feet, fans across the floor
and the fuzzy line rises on the wall,
over my head and up to the ceiling
        as I stand in the sky inside.

This Athena

walked through the valley
of the thief – death – touched
by fingertips cadaver cold,
icy bones clattering laughter
in disasters, the ravishment
of insatiably devouring void.

She did not stray.
She dove into this chasm,
the rift in our existence
where too many are lost.

She, clarion, "Everyone may live lives
of fulfillment, fountains
of overflowing abundance
upon which we all may rise."
She will give her life for this.
She cannot live without this.

Shade of Day

Too often life feels encrusted in cold
when the pitch darkness of uncertainty
blears and blights the radiant clarity
and ice bites everywhere we are exposed.
Light had extended distances now closed,
and foresight becomes only disparity
and hope staggers to collapse of frailty
as flowers wilt in a shadowy fold.
Being blind we nudge closer in our holds
learning to listen with each other's cries
as through touch we learn to open our eyes
and revive the life frozen stiff of old.
Then sadness imbues one's brightening face
as night is just another shade of day.

Children's Song (fragment)

On the days when I'm restless and bored
I walk the library corridors
and from the shelves I pull random books
to open them up for sudden looks
then watch the startled words awake
that had been sleeping on the page.

Talking with Plants

In a language of shape, color and scent
the swaying flowers said, "Come" and meant it.
Yet the thorns smartly pricked me to beware.
So I carefully reached to touch the fruit
that kissed my lips with syrupy "Thank You"s
and asked I spread word of what their seeds bear.

Extending from Within

Without imposing, there's no impression,
but how is one to go about without
obstructing? Is the interference
irresistible, an initial jerk,
obstinate as existence, corresponding
with time in a mesh of persistence?
Doesn't the smooth eventually slip?
Or is it always? With the infusion,
is there no identity? Without this,
is there any being? Idle wondering.
Are we tumbling in an indistinct blob
bloating oblivious oblivion?

Such inquiries go unheard, a careful
intricacy of considerations,
speculating upon the absurd,
increasingly abstract and detached,
expressed with exceptional eloquence
in a dark and empty room.
Impressing nothing. Pushing nothing away.

Strength

Lashed by ice spiked winds
and buried beneath stone frozen snow
he awakened like a flower.

Encased in a cast iron egg
he opened with dreamy wings
that embraced the entire sky.

Driven to the barren distance
and beaten to the ground
he rose like the sun.

Persephone

Attentive of the contents
culminating from all her life
throughout all that she extends
she hands him the meticulous
gift with a budding urge to burst,
hoping that he will take the time
to untie the intricate lines
of her carefully composed mind
and see how the poem turns out.

Kipling (sketch)

At either side of accumulated
elevation amassed on the basis
that spans the reaches of the common place,
many hope for some moment of grandeur
lost in the wonders of discovery
or the austere esteem of humility.

The jut of a bare bluff into the sky
overlooking the lay of the land
undulating with the ripples of time
as the verdure breathes the different seasons.
Then standing above the setting sun
cowled in hues of its brilliant solitude
nodding in resolve beneath the surface,
watch the stars arrive, singularly
and then innumerably wheel around
the fixture of a clear cynosure.

Or along the shores of thorny brambles,
following a purling stream's ascent
and each step approaching the distant roar
until the moment it suddenly opens
with the dazzling sight of the water
exhaustlessly leaping from the edge
of a stern, steep cliff softened with dripping moss,
as the mist drifts through the rainbow's archway
above the refreshment of emerald pools.

Or in the lush fern creases of ravines
discovering the vine veined entrances
of cavernous temples yawning openings
leading into the primordial dark
beckoning ventures into the quiet deep.

Yet to reach these places evoked along
the overgrown paths of lore, folk rumors
from the visits of mysterious strangers,
their steps are through the slogs of mud,
the whistling of wind in open vistas
is more the snarls of briars and slides of scree.
Yet beyond the anguish of these weary,
blind struggles taunted with suffering loss
we seek the wonders we could never foresee.

Object of Memory

Everyone has a favorite image,
even in the varied shapes of touch and taste.
The smiling face of someone they hold dear,
the swinging open of their own front door,
people admiring their polished car out front
or an infant giggling and waving mirth
from the plush ruffles of a secure crib.

In my twenties I loved alluvial fans,
the dry deposits, the remnants of wash
and the promise of the wash's return.
I never thought of mountains melting,
but rather the mountains turning inside out,
opening themselves over the valleys
beneath the cloudless desert skies.

Brecht's Alabama

I caught myself saying something of the sorts
(sets extending and connecting in every direction)
reckoning what the topic might boil down to
and I thought to build upon the folk colloquial
in an erudite and sophisticated direction
with the precision equipment of an alembic,
but then I thought again and reckoned I wasn't
concerned with what boiled down and thought
I'd show my roots and turn from the rotten mash
and ascend with the vapors that turned
in the cooling coils of copper tube and drip
in mason jars with the shine of the moon.

Sketch

Imagining a painter through a vague
distance of solitude, working in what
appears to be a haphazardly splattered
studio, sitting in a swivel chair
surrounded by a crowd of canvases
standing and whispering among themselves
on the subject of the invisible
increments, always beginning from a blank,
extending the steady tip of a brush
to place one delicate dab of paint
after another, considering the hues
and their correspondence brushed through air
from palette to palate as each touch is placed
within the proportions of the canvas'
stretched edge as an image slowly assembles.

Messenger

The Mercurial steps
stride through the open air
where round ripples
outstretch the distance
with myriad reflections
of magnetic music.

I see Grand Central's clock
and the Empire State building
flexing his stout shoulders
and blowing colorful kisses
to the elegant Chrysler Building
with her sparkling corolla crown.

From the Embrace

In those oppressive moments alone,
when the world cringes and recoils
from even the most tender touch,
my mind embarks on a peripatetic
stroll with Aristotle to view the world
through the descriptions of his mind
translated through vast spans of time,
or Virginia Woolf takes my hand
and leads me through the personal
thoughts and impressions
of an assembled cast of characters
as if we were swimming through the waves
of oceans and feeling the subtle changes
of temperature and the turns of currents
as we pass through the embrace
of one body of water after another
so that I feel more prepared to accept
the inconclusiveness of existence.

Limerick

In scolding tones he had been told,
"Drive on the right side of the road!"
but found this mistaken
when visiting Britain,
so he left to think on his own.

Out Lines

Surrounded by invisible mountains
they are pressed with a sense of the unseen.
There is no certainty if the challenge
is an obstruction or reluctance,
but the temptation to stay is sweet,
suckling the abundance
dripping from a sow's teat
and swell themselves
into what they may become.
They do know, it is better to choose
and be wrong, than not choose at all.

They may push upon the mountains,
but these mountains do not move.
They may point them out to others,
but they cannot be seen.
So they climb into the open sky
where they are recognized
in the trace of their outlines.

The Ensemble of the Audience

In their places, they heard in their own way,
compelled from their friends' recommendations,
encountering posts in their life's stations,
or while reading reviews in the paper,
all suggesting that they must see the show.
They assembled as complete strangers,
converging from their diverse histories
and the broad assortment of roles
they play on each private and professional stage.
Coinciding their lives at curtain time
to witness the agonizing trials of life
and the elating amusements of inspiration
they sit in agreement as the audience
as each uniquely enjoys the performance.

After the Storm

Whoever has never been kicked around
in life, has never bothered to be born.
Countless times I have gathered my scattered
papers in the rain while watching the ink
bleed into bleak oblivion. I have
staggered from motley recollections
of my folly, reminded of my being
by pain, my love by heartbreak, the comforts
of home by the severity of loss
while only receiving recognition
in other's disdain. My declarations
become obscured with the uncertainty
of each flit situation, leaving me
to insist, and insist by doing it,
that while I breath, I will continue to sing,
plunging through the mirages and delusions,
holding a ground from which I took shape,
until, from a distance, I witness
Yeats' pouring over an open tome,
his spectacles sparkling with candle light
as he painstakingly tunes
his phrases into musical language.

Melting Point

I have seen dances before
and melted mercury cool
and spilled out onto the floor
into a quivering pool.

If there is a reflection
that anyone else can see
it would be from a tense surface
rippling in sweet agony

as I outstretch my existence
so my whole life is a feeling,
not of the thinnest possession,
but a touch throughout extending.

Then being poured, I am transformed
through the supple shapes of each performance,
uplifted within the inspiration borne
while endlessly falling in love with dance.

Mount Blank
— For Stephen Crane

This ledge may do nothing but narrow.
The whipping wind pries one from the stone,
passing careless as the mountain's stillness,
an immensity of indifference.
One knows there is no peak to reach, there is
no height upon which one may set oneself
with a surmounting sense of expanse and conquest.
There is nothing to this life but the desperate climb
with no direction but to cling for one's life
or turn back and plunge to one's death.
One could have chosen to graze in the rolling
meadows below, however one knows:
inspiration is not in a flowery breeze,
but in the gasping breath of harrowing fatigue.

Whale

In
another
element, I
have watched
leviathans glide.
Their songs do not
reach my ears. I
have never felt,
nor have I been
embraced with
the sonorous
shapes of their
perceptive
waves.
Instead,
I lean
over
a
rail
above
their trails
of bubbly breath
as they fly through the
condensation of the sky
.

Five

The New Atlantis

Through my life, I have been self-absorbed with existence.
I have believed our civilization is of great consequence,
that our vehicles must scatter seeds into the universe
to ensure that life survives.
                              The conviction is inevitable.
I can only see with my own eyes. Even extended
through a telescopic device, my sight is nothing more
than what may be imposed upon the resolution of my mind.
Then, feeling the sand beneath my feet, I realize
our civilization is a single grain on the long beach
at this moment aligned with the Milky Way.
Then I think that behind the curtain lapping at the shore,
through the soft ruffles of the curling, twirling surf,
deepening beneath the quieting sea,
mollusks are busy building the new Atlantis.

A Sonnet for the Sonnet

Being a sonneteer, I am enamored
by sonnets, but today to my delight
serendipity favored me to find
a university class that explored
the passionate history of the form.
The lecture described this frame tumbling through lives,
uniting affections through centuries of time.
There is no language that it scorns;
there is no culture it cannot adorn.
This delicate and vigorous design
turns eternal in awakening minds
and endures with the desires it records.
I swear with my life and the lute I strum,
as long as we love sonnets will be sung.

Soul

Often, I become discombobulated.
My thoughts whirl in one direction
while my body lunges in another
and I fall into a heap between.
Such times I seek a cathedral
where Bach is playing inside
to tune the harmonics of flesh and life.

The Child

The child can pick up anything
and release it anywhere.
The tangible and the fantastic are one
in the immensity of the imagination.

A tiny twig transforms into a ship
bobbing along the currents of a river
on its way to cross oceans.
The stone skips over a lake
and the further it hops,
the deeper it sinks, submarine.

The child can lift a car
and hover it over any terrain,
place a building on a moon,
build castles in the clouds.

The child can arrange a tea party
where the regal mingle
with next door neighbors,
politely discussing delicacies
while sipping tea from a kettle
that pours exhaustless thought.

Home Is in His Head

His house's exterior is so modest
and the demands of the world outside
are so distracting, he practically forgot
the palatial expanses inside.
For most of his time, he had filled the corridors
of his life with the intricacies of his interests
and rediscovers what he had left to support
only after stumbling back from a long absence.
He opens the drapes and brightens the space,
filling the chambers with light and breeze,
and sets about to freshen the place
and entertain whomever his fancies please.
We are often lost in our search to engage,
and forget the best way is in how we accommodate.

Synecdoches and Self

Visiting an exhibit portraying
the ways we communicate, I tiptoed
along the walls that stood around the crowd
that gathered with their backs to the paintings
while roiling contently in contention.
The frames were filled with genitals and fists.
I heard some argue that it is coitus
that sustains us, others — manipulation.

Their voices receded as I walked deeper
down the halls past corridors opening
away from the fray with welcoming space.
Then I climbed a winding stair
to the lines and shape of understanding
in the delicate sketch of a human face.

57038372R00066

Made in the USA
Charleston, SC
02 June 2016